An Anthology out of South Africa

Second Edition

An Anthology out of South Africa

An Anthology out of South Africa

Second Edition

Published by

William Jenkins

2503-4288 Grange Street
Burnaby, BC Canada V5H 1P2

williamhenryjenkins@gmail.com

http://www.williamjenkins.ca

Telephone: 1-778-953-6139

ISBN: 1928164137
ISBN-13: 978-1-928164-13-5

An Anthology out of South Africa

Table of Contents

Acknowledgement

The photo on the cover of this edition is courtesy The Letaba Herald. It shows Managing Editor Lukas Groenewaki in the act of purchasing a copy of the book from each of three of the authors, Jackey Mukhawana, Alter Mathebula and Eustacia Nhlangweni. Not present for the photo was author Bekazi Mboweni.

Mr. Groenewaki acted as recipient of copies of the second edition that were printed in Capetown, South Africa after we had difficulties getting proof copies to Jackey. He also interviewed the authors and printed an article in the Letaba edition of the Herald.

This local support of these budding writers, all learners at Hudson Ntsan'wisi Senior Secondary School in Nkowankowa, Letaba, Limpopo Province, South Africa is very much appreciated.

An Endorsement

Words are powerful tools that can be used for the benefit of humanity or for its downfall. Words can be inspiring and they can be heartbreaking. Words fill us with knowledge that can change our lives in a second. But when words are used as the instruments of conscious poetry, they harmonise the knowledge with the resonance of truth and affect our consciousness on many levels.

I fully support William Jenkins, in Vancouver, Canada, in his effort to publish stories and poems written by South African Secondary School students and his efforts to expose the tool of enslavement called money. He believes that every contribution helps and encourages others to find their way to help mankind end our obsession with money.

Michael Tellinger - Founder of the UBUNTU Liberation Movement and UBUNTU Party.
Waterval Boven, South Africa.

MICHAEL TELLINGER
UBUNTU Contributionism
A World Without Money

Preface

This book of stories, poems and plays written by secondary school students in South Africa grew out of a contact by Jackey Mukhawana of Limpopo Province. He found my earlier website or found me on Facebook.

In any case, he wrote and asked if I would publish his writing. After some negotiation, I agreed to look at his story "My Life, My Misery", a rags-to-riches fairy tale that he produced in installments using his cell phone as a typewriter. He would email each chapter to me and I would make minor edits to correct obvious spelling mistakes.

Since his story took up only a few pages, I added a section where readers could draw the scene being described or add more description or details. When it was ready, I submitted it to Creatspace.com for production as a paperback book. I also submitted it to Kindle for him.

I ordered four copies of the paperback, sent two to Jackey on December 24th, 2014, sent one copy to the Legal Deposit section of the Library of Canada and kept one copy for my archives. It took three months for the books to arrive at Jackey's post box.

I asked Jackie to send me more writing and to encourage his fellow students to write as well. He has sent me a couple of plays, another story and two poems of which one play and one poem were by classmates.

In order to attempt to get more submissions, I wrote a note offering to make a small payment for each acceptable poem, play or story. Finally, I started receiving submissions, mostly by Jackey, but also from three of his friends. I limited the number I could accept as that's all I could afford at that time. Edition 2 reorganizes these writings by author and includes some additional work that the students have sent me.

Jackey Mukhawana

Jackey Mukhwana is a high school student at Hudson Ntsan'wisi Senior Secondary School in Nkowankowa, Letaba, Limpopo Province, South Africa. He was born in 1999 in Tzaneen (Dan Village) where he lives with his parents and a younger sister and brother. From an early age he has loved helping people and he enjoys playing with his siblings and teaching them to read. He found that he liked writing when in Grade 7 and has been pecking away at his cell phone, writing short stories, dredged from his vivid imagination and life experiences.

Jackey believes that his calling in life is to be a heart surgeon, someone who can help people suffering from heart disease. He expects to continue writing short stories and will publish a few more in 2015.

My Life, My Misery

Chapter 1

In a not-so-far-away village there once lived a boy named Kidan who had no one in his life. His parents had been found beaten up and dead in the house and his other family members could not be located.

Rumours started spreading that Kidan was responsible for the death of his parents. Everyone hated him. They called him a demon. Parents wouldn't let their children play with him. They would tell their children that he killed his parents and that he would kill them if they played with him.

With no one to take care of him, Kidan had to learn to take care of himself at the age of fourteen. Kidan understood that he was not wanted by anyone. Whenever he entered the street, everyone would hide away. Sometimes they would throw stones at him saying that he was a demon and that he should die.

Kidan had a voice. He could sing. Every evening he would sing his self-made songs about his miserable life. The villagers would call his songs demonic without listening to the message.

One day, one man decided to call a meeting. At the meeting, he told the other villagers that Kidan should be banished from the village because he was a danger to everyone. All of them agreed.

That evening, all the male villagers went to Kidan's place and chased him out. From a distance away, Kidan saw his house burn down. He had no choice but to leave. "Where can I go?" is the question he asked himself.

Chapter 2

Kidan started his journey to an unknown destination. Walking, walking, walking without stopping and no food. He passed many villages asking for jobs, but nobody cared. Some villagers would even set the dogs on him.

As he sat under the shadows of the tall trees in the forest where he found he had to live, he felt as though the world had turned against him. Every day, Kidan continued walking always hoping that someday he would be accepted and that everything would be okay.

There was a time when Kidan felt like giving up, but his treasure kept him going. His voice was his treasure, a treasure no one ever liked. It was a treasure he was afraid to show.

He believed that one day his treasure would shine like the treasure of diamonds in the sky.

No matter what happened he would sing a song in his heart that said "Never stop believing".

Chapter 3

After a long time of misery, Kidan came up with a plan. He decided to use his voice, but he wondered "Will anyone admire my singing or will they also call me a demon".

One afternoon, in the village in which Kidan was living, a daughter of the richest man in the village, Lucia, was taking a walk through the forest when she heard a very beautiful, magical voice. Lucia wanted to see the person singing with such a beautiful voice. She started looking, walking towards the sound of the voice. When Lucia saw that it was Kidan singing, she could not believe her eyes. A handsome young man with very dirty clothes was singing to himself.

She started talking to him. These two became good friends. Lucia would secretly bring food to Kidan and they would sing together every day.

One afternoon, her father ordered one of his guards to follow Lucia. When the guard told her father what he saw, he ordered the other guards to bring Kidan to him. Kidan was beaten up like a dog and told to leave the village immediately. The following day, when Lucia went to their secret place, no one was there. Kidan had left the village in pain.

As he was traveling, only Lucia's face appeared in his mind. He made a promise to himself that he would come back for her. He realized that he could not go back without any money. He had to do something.

Chapter 4

Eventually, Kidan ended up in an unusual place with mysterious things that he had never seen in any of the villages he had passed through. There were tall buildings, some so tall that he felt as if they were falling over, and beautiful clothing that he had never seen before.

Kidan started looking for a job but no one would hire an uneducated peasant. Kidan was very sad, sitting under a tree in the beautiful park of the mysterious place that all these people called a city, when an old man appeared before him holding a guitar. He gave the guitar to Kidan and said "Learn to use your gift. Only then will you be able to live the life of your dreams".

Kidan could not understand, but before he could ask any questions, the old man was already a distance away.

Chapter 5

Kidan started learning how to play the guitar. He was amazed by the way he could play the instrument and sing to the sound it made.

One morning, as he was walking, he saw a poster of a competition. It said that the winner would get a lot of money. Kidan didn't believe in himself; he didn't believe he could make it. One nice lady came past him and she stopped. She asked "Are you a musician?"

Kidan could not answer. Then, she told him that he should enter this competition. No holding back, he must believe in himself, not be shy, stand up, talk and believe that the world is his. These words empowered Kidan in a huge way.

He decided to enter the competition, but when he reached the stage, because of his appearance, the audience began to "boo" at him. This almost brought him down, but he remembered the woman's words.

When he started singing, the booing transformed to cheering. Kidan taught these people not to judge a book by its cover.

Kidan won the competition. Every recording company wanted to work with him. He was taken to school, taught everything about the big city.

Kidan now had the life he never dreamt of, but there was something missing, Lucia. He decided to go back to the village where Lucia stayed, and the first place he went was their secret place. A distance away he heard her singing their song. He then joined in.

Lucia could not believe her ears and eyes. Before her stood a handsome, clean, rich man. At that moment, she knew it really was him, Kidan. Lucia's father and Kidan made peace. The two young people married and set off to the city to live there.

Kidan knew he had to make peace with his own villagers. By the time he returned to the village, they already realized that they had made a huge mistake. When he arrived with his cars and introduced himself as Kidan, they knew they had to apologize, but did not know how to do it. They all started crying, rolling on the ground, begging for forgiveness. Kidan's words were "I hold no grudges with anyone. Let us forget the past and live in the present and anticipate the future."

Kidan was a very well-known singer all over the world. He knew the life in the streets and so he built a shelter for all the homeless. He asked companies to help out in supplying food. There never was a person with such a golden heart as Kidan had.

My Boyfriend, My Destroyer

Copyright © Jackey Mukhawana 2015

Chapter 1

My name is Navel. October the 14th, 1998 is the date of my birth. I am the only child of John and Sophia Mixtelpuktem who live in a small village in the heart of Africa. My parents are very poor.

As I grew up, I was a very bright learner at school. My teachers always said that I had a bright future ahead of me, but how can I have a bright future if I have no money to further my studies?

One day as I was walking home after school, a very fancy beautiful car stopped beside me. An older guy was driving. He looked as if he was in his late 20's. He introduced himself as Michael and asked for my name. He even offered me a ride home and I accepted the lift.

On the way home, he told me that I was a very beautiful young girl and that any man would be very lucky to have me as a friend. At first I took it as a compliment, but as he went on and on about my beauty and loveliness, I knew he was up to something. Then he touched my cheek and told me that he loved me and that he wanted to be my boyfriend.

Before I could say anything, he took out a big bundle of money and handed it to me. I didn't want anything to do with this, but then I thought about my need for money to further my studies. He told me that by loving him I would get anything my heart desired.

As a young naive girl, I said yes to his proposal. Every day Michael would come over after school and take me home. He always dropped me off a distance away from home so that my parents wouldn't get suspicious.

I developed a lot of love for money to the extent that I couldn't control myself. Whenever he took me shopping, I would buy all the expensive things.

One day when he fetched me from school, the trip was unlike others. He didn't drop me off where he usually did. Instead, he drove away with me. When I asked why he didn't drop me off, he just smiled and told me that I would love what was about to happen. I got really excited thinking that he might buy me something lovely or take me somewhere special. We stopped at a big, beautiful hotel. We booked a room and ordered food and drinks. I was allowed to order anything I wanted.

After a few hours, Michael started acting all strange. He told me about my beauty and how beautiful I would be if only I took off my clothes. At first I didn't want to do it, but he was very persuasive and he convinced me to take off my clothes because it was only the two of us in the room. I did as I was told and didn't think of the worst. No!

I didn't know about the worst. I thought that this was the love that everyone talks about. I thought it was love when he did it. He raped me.

Chapter 2

After he raped me, I felt very different as though something had been taken from me. Michael just laughed and said I would get used to it. He took me home, but it was so late my parents had gotten very worried. I knew that if I told my parents where I had been, I would be punished. I lied to them for the first time. I told my parents that I had been studying at school and that I hadn't seen the time fly.

Michael started buying me food for the whole month every month. He also bought me a brand new smartphone. My parents wanted to know where I got the money to buy all these things. Whenever they asked about this issue, I would ignore them and just walk away. Sometimes when they would ask me to do something, I'd just grab my "cool" phone and start chatting online or just tell them I was tired. They got very annoyed because of my attitude. Finally, they kicked me out of the house.

I didn't worry because I knew that Michael would take care of me. I now lived in a hotel. In the beginning, I would go to school every day, but as time went on I could no longer see the need of education in my life. I left school and started clubbing every night.

I made new friends and started doing drugs and smoking. This was the dream of most girls. Michael liked my new lifestyle and I also enjoyed it too.

One day I went back to my old school. The teachers were very surprised to see me, but I didn't care. When they tried talking to me, I just told them that I'm not one of the "stupids" in the classroom. I told them that life was about taking chances. I went to every classroom when no teacher was present and I told all the girls to follow in my footsteps. They could tell that I was living an amazing life because of the way I was dressed. I was only 17, but I was living a life of a princess.

10

Life tasted sweeter than honey to me. My parents wanted me to become like them, but I rejected them and followed my own path.

One evening at a night club, a woman came to me angrily and told me to take my filthy body elsewhere. I didn't understand at first, but she then called me ugly names and told me to leave her man alone. I laughed at her and turned away.

Oh hell. She didn't let me be. She turned me around and slapped my face. I lost my mind for a few seconds, but I couldn't let her get away with what she had done. We then fought until the people in the club called it a night and stopped us from fighting. I was very angry. As soon as I arrived at the hotel, I called Michael, asking him to come over. He probably knew what had happened because he refused to come.

The following evening, Michael came. He told me that the woman was just crazy. He said that he was not involved with anyone besides me. I believed him; after all I was just a naive young girl.

Chapter 3

One night a few weeks later, I almost died. A group of women came to my hotel room holding guns. They told me to leave Michael alone or else their boss, who was just standing behind them with her scary face and fancy clothes, would kill me. They told me to leave him or I'd kiss my life goodbye.

I tried fighting them, but only got myself into trouble that was a million times worse for me. I was beaten up, hurt badly, and left on the floor bleeding like a dog with no owner.

The next day, Michael came over, only to find me lying on the floor in great pain. He quickly took me to the hospital where I was kept in bed for days. On the day I was to be discharged, the doctor told me the worst unbelievable words, ones I never dreamt of hearing.

He told me that I was pregnant, but that was no problem.

He also told me that I was now H.I.V. active. It felt as though that moment was a nightmare dressed up in a reality suit.

Michael later came to fetch me. I could not breath a word out on the way to the hotel. When he left me at the hotel, I knew I had a lot to think about. So many questions piled in my mind. What would I do if he left me with the baby? What would he do to me when he found out I was H.I.V. positive? Where would I go? My life would be ruined. I almost died because of him. I could not lose him that easily.

A week of thinking passed. I decided to tell him about my pregnancy because even if I didn't tell him, he would still notice. I was so proud of the joy he showed when I told him. He even took me out for dinner that evening. I was very happy thinking that the baby would grow our bond even stronger.

He proposed to marry me. He knelt on one knee and said a song of forever lasting love "WILL YOU MARRY ME?" A moment of silence and tears of joy, I said "yes" and that was just the happiest moment of my life.

Chapter 4

Days later, Michael told me that he needed to leave the country for some business and that he would be back after two weeks. I knew he was working very hard for the future of our baby. He promised to call me every day until he came back. He then took his leave.

Days passed, no call, no text, no nothing. The whole two weeks passed with no word from Michael. The end of the month came. I was surprised when the hotel manager came to my room and told me that my payment hasn't been made and that I was given only one hour to pack up my stuff and go.

Things were now falling apart. It had been two years of fun, and it had all come to an end. I was only 18 and pregnant, with the H.I.V. in my blood. I had nowhere to go. I was afraid to go home. I spent the cold night in the streets with no money.

The following day, I went home. All my former school mates had graduated and set off to varsity. When I arrived at home, my mother could not believe her eyes. She felt as though she was in dream land. When my father came out of the house, his eyes were fixed right at me. I could see the anger and betrayal in his eyes, combined with the pain I've caused in my mother's eyes. They wanted nothing to do with me. They told me they had no child. They said I was dead to them. My tears fell like "THE BLACK EVIL RAIN". I begged for their forgiveness. I had now realised the gigantic blunder I'd made. I explained the whole story on my knees in a flash. I saw my mother break down and burst into tears when I mentioned that I was pregnant. They let me in and told me that I could stay, but I knew it would take time for the wounds in their hearts to heal.

Chapter 5

Months later, I had become a mother. With no job and no husband, I had to find a way to raise my baby girl with love and care. I even thought of prostitution, but I would only be living my previous life. I started attending church and found my hidden talent of singing. I always sang at church to praise God. A night adult school opened. I was given a second chance and used it wisely. I studied very hard. Thinking of my baby, my health and my parents, I knew I had to work very hard to make up for all the time I had thrown away. At age 22, I finished my high school studies and was recognised by the government who offered to pay for my studies. I studied medicine. At age 29, I had become a doctor. My parents were very proud of me.

My life was almost destroyed by a person I thought of building a future with. It has been five years since I became a doctor and my daughter is 14 years old. Just by looking at her, she convinced me to go around schools advising young girls about the dangers of "sugar daddies" to young girls

Note: Stay safe, have self-respect and love who you are. It might be hard today, but that doesn't mean you should give your whole life away to men. To those young girls with kids, life goes on. You can still reach your dreams, just as I reached mine. Just don't make the same mistakes over and over. "Two mistakes don't make it right"

Royalty.

Chapter 1

Being a princess is every young girl's dream.

My name is Blessing, I am a princess. I was named Blessing because I am the only daughter of King Alendo and Queen Natalia of Shawndy Kingdom. All my life I lived by royalty rules. My father was often away; he would come back home once or twice a month.

As a teenager, I went to school as any other teenager did. I got whatever I wanted whenever I wanted it. Well, not everything. I always wanted to be free, just like any other person, but I was treated differently.

My mother would always say "You are not like all the other girls who go out anywhere they want anytime. You are a princess and you must be well-protected. And yes, you must also get married to a well-educated Prince and be well taken care of, as you deserve."

I could not understand the difference in me. Whenever I went to the mall, I always had a guard with me. I never understood why life was like this for royalty. One day after school, I did not wait for my driver to take me home. I went to the mall alone. I wanted to know the feeling of being alone in the mall. I had ice cream, and tried on some beautiful clothes in the clothing stores. I really had fun, but it wasn't long until the royal guards were turning the mall up-side-down searching for me.

My mother was very upset. "Blessing, do you know how unsafe you were?" she asked in tears. "You scared me, young lady."

I knew I had to let my feelings out.

"Mother," I said, sadly, "I am still young. I know that I am a princess, but I'm also human and I deserve to be free. Mother, with all the respect you deserve, may I please go to the mall alone anytime I like? Before you can answer, allow me to tell you that I had a lot of fun alone," I said with a smile on my face.

My mother could see the spark of joy in my eyes.

"You have made your point, princess. You are now free to visit the mall alone anytime you wish to do so, but your father must not hear anything about this. Now go and freshen up, then come back. After dinner, I have something big to tell you," she said with a smile.

I could not wait to hear what she was to tell me. I went upstairs and had a bath that was prepared for me.

After dinner, my mother asked my brothers to excuse us and they left us alone. She then moved from her seat and came and sat next to me. She looked at me and smiled. I could not help but anticipate on hearing what was behind her lips. But before she could spell out a word, one of the royal maids came in and said "My Queen, you have guests."

I was highly disappointed because mother had to see her guests.

"Darling, let me attend to my guests. We'll talk later. I will send for you when I'm done,"

She walked away in her royal red and white long dress.

Chapter 2

Mother did not call me that night.

The following morning when I woke up, my eldest brother, the crown prince, told me that my mother had left for Danville kingdom to support her dear friend Queen Elisa, because her son, the crown prince had gone missing. It was a good thing that she did, but I also wanted to know what she wanted to tell me. That afternoon, I was watching a hospital program, and was so touched by seeing all those sick people. I asked my driver to take me to the local hospital. I went room to room greeting all the sick people and wishing them a fast recovery. Of all the stories they told me, only one hit my heart deeply. A very handsome young man was sitting alone and lonely in one of the rooms. I entered the room hoping to put a smile on his face.

"Good day," I said as I greeted him with a smile.

"Hello," he replied happily. "Do you by any chance know who I am?"

I was confused.

"The only thing I remember is my name. My name is A.J.; that is all I remember. I was involved in a plane crash and all my belongings were turned to ashes, together with the other passengers. With nothing left, it is even harder to be identified."

I could not help but feel sorry and sad for him as he spoke. Each time he said a word, it seemed as though a knife was forced deeper into my heart. I ended up in tears imagining how he could be feeling at that moment.

"No, beautiful one," he said, holding my hand in his.

"Do not cry; it doesn't suit your lovely face," he said looking at me with a smile.

I wiped my tears and said to him "No human deserves that, but what has happened, has happened. Let's just hope you will be able to remember in time."

Every day I would pay him a visit. After a month, my mother, the Queen came back to Shawndy palace. By this time, I had already fallen in love with A.J.

Days after she came back, she was sitting outside under the mango tree in our backyard having a glass of juice. She called me and asked me to join her.

"Princess," she called, "now that you are eighteen years old, I think it's time I let you out into the light; it's time for you to know the truth."

I could not understand.

"What truth, mother?"

She looked at me for a second then looked away.

"My child, I am sure you never understood why you were always kept indoors. Well, here is the answer you've been looking for. When you were born, the royal family of Danville asked for your hand in marriage so you would be the future queen of Danville kingdom. It was all agreed and it was just about time for you to get married when Afrom-Junior disappeared."

I looked straight into mother's eyes.

"Mother..."

She stopped me before I could say a word.

"I am not done, listen. Since you cannot get married to Afrom-Junior, another crown prince of the land of green, also known as Nature Kingdom, asked for your hand in marriage."

I could not believe what my ears were hearing. I stood up and shouted "No, mother, no."

"Do not raise your voice at me, young lady," Mother said with a firm voice.

"Mother, how can you expect me to marry someone I don't even know?" I asked, upset.

"How many times must I tell you that you are royal? You are nothing like all the other girls. All royal princesses marry princes chosen for them. You can't argue with that, it's final. You will marry the prince of Nature Kingdom."

She stood up and started walking away.

"I will not, mother. I have already found the person I love and want to spend the rest of my life with him."

I said these words crying.

She turned infuriated and walked back to the mango tree where I was standing. She slapped me for the first time in my life.

"I have never been this disappointed in my life," she said in tears. "I did everything you asked me to do. I even went behind your father's back by letting you have a little freedom. I did not know that I was just digging a grave for myself. From now on, your only outing will be to school. No more mall, and certainly, no more hospital. That is final."

She walked away.

I fell on the ground crying. I didn't know what to do because I really loved A.J.

"Father is coming home tomorrow. We'll see what he'll say about this," I shouted.

Mother stopped walking, but did not look back. Then, she continued walking and went into the house.

Chapter 3

The king came back the following day. Trumpets were blowing, drums were hit, royal guards marching beside the king's cars as they enter the palace. I remember one of the elders welcoming the king. "Bow for the arrival of his royal highness, welcome the royal king with a bow. Oh-hail King Alendo of Shawndy Kingdom. Oh-hail King Alendo.

That very same evening, mother and father called me to their room and asked me to sit on the veranda with them.

"My daughter, your mother told me something very unpleasant. She told me that you now no longer want to follow the royal rules," my father, the king said.

"Father, I respect you, but this rule of you choosing a husband for me is not fair," I said, hoping that father would understand.

He just sighed and shook his head.

"Princess, it has been like this for over a thousand years. Your mother was once a princess. At birth, my side of the family went to her kingdom to ask for her hand in marriage."

I knew that father was a hard nut to crack, but I had to try.

"But she didn't know until she was eighteen. Here is a question for the both of you. Did you love each other when you got married?"

My mother rushed to answer.

"Blessing, love comes after. You first get married then love will develop. That is the way of our culture."

"Mother, without love there is no happiness. Were you both pleased to marry someone you didn't know?" I asked looking straight into father's eyes.

"Princess, that doesn't matter. You will know each other as time goes on after you've gotten married. Now to more serious matters, I dislike the fact that you have fallen in love with a person who doesn't even know himself."

I looked at my father in disappointment.

"Father, you can't say that. It's not his fault that he can't remember himself. I love him. I cannot just kill the love I have for him. At least, think about my feelings."

Father showed a very unpleasant face then opened his mouth and said "I thought you knew better, but now I see that you are very stupid."

These words hurt me hard. I then ran out of the room in tears. I went to my room and locked myself inside. I cried the whole night non-stop. The following morning I was forced to go to the hospital and tell A.J. that I could no longer see him. Mother went there with me. But when we arrived, I wouldn't do it. It was very hard for me. I could not afford to break a broken person's heart.

"It's your choice. Either, you go inside and do what you have to do or we can stay here until you feel like it" Mother said.

I felt pain, serious pain. I then took a deep breath and went inside. A.J. was very pleased to see me when I entered the room. I pretended to be fine, but he had grown to know me.

"Oh my love, what is the problem? Even though you have a smile on your face, your eyes tell me that you're pretending."

I looked down and tears started rolling out of my eyes. When I tried opening my mouth, the pain got greater. I had to say it or my parents would not be happy at all.

"My parents don't want me to see you anymore because you are not royal and I have to marry a prince chosen for me by my father and the royal council."

He shook his head. He was about to say something when I ran out of the room in tears. I went straight to the car and asked to be taken home.

Chapter 4

Months had passed and I had to marry Prince Tom of the Nature kingdom. The wedding week came, but I still did not want to marry Tom. I decided to lock myself in my room. My mother came to my room five days before the wedding.

"Blessing, please open this door. We need to talk."

I only shouted "Go away."

I could hear the sadness in mother's voice as she spoke. "Princess, please I really miss you, my daughter, please. Your father misses you too. Please, darling, do the right thing. Your wedding is five days from today."

Her last words made me more emotional. I could not marry someone I didn't even know. I had to find a way to see my A.J. Just maybe we could run away together and spend the rest of our lives together.

That very same day mother came back to my room's door and knocked.

"Princess, I have good news. You won't marry Prince Tom anymore."

This brought joy to my heart.

"The reason is that Afrom-Junior returned to his home, meaning that you will be marrying him."

All that pain came back after these words. I did not want to be with anyone but A.J.

26

That very same evening when everyone was in their rooms, I ran for it. I made sure that none of the guards saw me as I sneaked out of the palace. I went to the hospital and got there right on time for visiting hours. But to my sadness, the nurses told me that A.J. had left. They told me that his family came for him. The pain got even greater due to the thought of never seeing the love of my life again. I collapsed right before the reception desk. The last thing I remembered when I woke up was my tears. I woke up on a hospital bed in the hospital and next to me were my parents.

"My baby, you are awake. We were very scared when we got a call from the hospital saying that you had fainted," said my mother. "But lucky us, you are okay."

The king, my father, said "I want to know who brought you here. Was it one of the guards? How could they do such a thing behind my back? I will make them pay," he continued.

"No, Father," I shouted. "Why does it seem that you have forgotten that I am human! Just to remind you, I am human and I can do things on my own. I am capable of walking myself to this hospital if you haven't noticed. Oh, I forgot. You are never around to witness your own children's feelings," I shouted and ended up in tears.

"Blessing, don't talk to your father like that. He might be your father, but he is still the king of this land. Now apologise," Mother spoke firmly.

"My deepest apology, father. It's just that A.J. has gone without saying goodbye."

27

They both pretended to be sad for me, but their joy was crystal clear. I could see right through them.

"Oh! Before I forget. The royal Family of Danville kingdom will be coming next week and Afrom-Junior will be coming along. We thought about what you said and we now see that you need to know someone before you can marry them, "Father said.

The doctor entered.

"Your highness, we have done some tests and the princess is okay. She's under a lot of stress. Being stressed is very dangerous, it can even lead to death and to someone her age it's much much more dangerous. I'd suggest you help her reduce her stress level," the doctor said.

Then my parents asked to take me home. They then filled some forms and later took me home.

Chapter 5

Two moons later, on a summer evening, I watched the afternoon giant star set, and the first night star appear with the moon by its side. For a moment, all my pains had gone away. That day I learned that nature is a weapon that one can use to fight internal pain. But just like any other moment, it passed and reality took hold. I could not suffer like that any longer. I made a promise to myself that I would try by all means to forget about A.J.

"I will make my parents proud, just as they raised me with love and care. They only wanted what was best for me. If marrying Afrom-Junior is what will make them happy, then that is what I will do, "I thought to myself.

Minutes later I went to the house, took a bath, ate dinner and went to bed. Five days passed. Finally, it was time to meet my husband to be. I was upstairs in my room when they arrived. I was sent for. As I walked down the stairs in my blue "delicious" dress, I saw the back of his head as he was walking into the dining room with everyone. I stopped on the stairs.

"Could it be?" I thought to myself. I was scared.

"My princess, they are waiting for you," the maid who was sent to call me reminded me that we did not have all night. We then continued our walk downstairs.

"No it can't be," I said, as I stopped at the door. He turned and looked at me.

"Beautiful one, you are the princess!"

I could not believe my ears and eyes. It was real. A.J. was really standing before me. It then all came clear to mind, A.J. for Afrom-Junior. The parents did not understand. We ran into each other's arms.

"Can someone tell me what is going on here?" King Afrom asked in confusion.

"Yes what is going on here?" my father asked in the same state of confusion.

A.J. and I just laughed. Then I told them everything about Afrom-Junior being the A.J. who they forced me to leave. They apologised and I forgave them.

When I started telling this story, did I say I am a princess? Oops! I made a blunder, I'm not a princess, but a Queen of Danville Kingdom. King A.J. and I now have a daughter. I don't think I need to tell you how I'm going to raise her up because you certainly have the picture painted in your mind already.

Keep reading. You might end up reading the story of her life someday.

My Best Friend, only for a few months

Copyright © Jackey Mukhawana 2015

A mysterious world this is, filled with surprises each single day. We know when our birthdays are, but never know our death date. We can have fun with a brother on this hour, and the next we get a call or announcement about his death. Life is a creature undefined, filled with surprises. You know when it starts, but never know when it will end. A confusing thing it is. That is life for you.

My name is Hudan. I am a business woman in a world called "Jackey's world". I want to tell you about my life as a teenager. I was a very shy, young girl. Growing up for me was not as sweet as honey. In fact, I spent my time dreaming of a bright future filled with all my heart's desires. My parents were among the less fortunate people in the community. My father worked in a farm and as little as he made, we would try and make a living out of it.

I didn't have a friend in my life. The only friends I had were described by men in my books. All that changed when I reached grade 10. Finally, I met someone I called a naturally-made friend. He was new in our school and attended the same class as I did. His name was Kimberly. Kimberly was the shy type. He spent most of his time alone and had no friends, just like me.

One day he found me at the passageway to the school toilets being bullied by those acclaimed mademoiselles of the kindergarten. He had the chance to turn a blind eye to what was happening, yet he chose to stop and asked exactly what was happening. Those wenches answered rudely, but oh yes, he kept his "cool". He threatened to report them to

31

the principal if they did not let me be. Knowing that the admonishment they would procure would not be an amiable one, they called us losers and departed. How gentle of him; he made sure that I was well.

From that day, Kimberly and I became best friends. I called him Kim and he called me Hud.

Whenever I was with with him, I felt that the world stood still. The fact that I was his only friend and he was my only friend just settled well in the depth of my heart. He was the brother I never had. I would often complain about my background, but Kim would not let me. He would always say "appreciate what you have because you never know how egregious life is for the person behind you".

No one had ever encouraged me to study as much as he did. He would assign me ten pages to read each single day and each following morning he would have a set of questions based on what I had studied. He and I became the best grade 10 learners and we fell in total love with our books. We spent almost all our time studying. We were the stars of mid-year exams and won trophies for being the zenith achievers of grade 10.

Life was sweet for that year, my grade 10 year, when I had someone to appreciate when life was not as sweet as I would like it to be.

Things got bad in the month of September when my best friend, Kim, got very sick. He was so sick that he would sometimes lose his ability to speak. Each time he spoke to me, he would ask me not to cry because he would be fine. I would read him my stories each time I went to see him in the hospital.

Kimberly was getting better. We enjoyed each other's company like crazy. We bonded like he was my brother and I was his sister. I came to the conclusion that he would get better and that he would come back to school and everything would be back on the right track.

One day, on a Saturday on the fifth of September, it was Kim's birthday and I had bought him a cake. I entered the hospital with smiles and red cheeks. When I reached the passageway to his room, I found his family sitting on the chairs with his mother and sister in tears. It felt like a dream. I was confused. I ran to his room like a mad chicken. Oh no! His room was empty.

What had happened here? I then ran out of the room and pulled his older brother off the chair where he was sitting in tears. I shouted "Where is my Kim?". One look explained it all. My first and only best friend was gone.

They say "Let bygones be bygones", but accepting this for me was very hard. I felt as though a part of me had been cut off.

I cried and cried and cried until I finally took a decision to study hard. I chose to make him proud. I studied as he had taught me.

Forever will Kimberly remain in my heart. May your soul rest in peace, Kimberly.

Life is too short. Death can strike at any time. Make your mark now, just as Kimberly did.

All's Well That Ends Well

Copyright © Jackey Mukhawana 2012 - 2015

Characters in the play

Jackey male
Lung-star female
Nashel female
Babiecha female
EX male
Vanessa female
Carrey female
Tofio male
Miss Mya female

Scene 1

(Miss Mya enters the classroom)

Miss Mya: Good morning.
Everyone: Morning, Miss.
Miss Mya: Today we will be learning about the sexual transmitted infections. Since you are teenagers, you are at a very high risk of coming in contact with them. Before we can start, may someone please tell me what Sexually Transmitted Infections mean?
(Only Lung-star raises her hand)
Miss Mya: What about the rest of you?
Babiecha: We are just not interested in your silly lesson.
Miss Mya: Young lady, you'll get a serious punishment if you don't stop this behaviour.
Babiecha: Whatever. (chewing a gum)

34

Miss Mya: That's it! I've had enough of your nonsense. I'm reporting you to the principal.

(Miss Mya walks out of the classroom)

Babiecha: (stands up) Nashel, Vanessa, let's get out of here. I've had enough of that silly teacher's nonsense. She thinks she knows everything.

Carrey: But she does know everything. She teaches...

Babiecha: Hey, hey, hey, keep it to yourself little miss know it all. No one was talking to you. Girls, let's roll.

(a couple of minutes later, Miss Mya walks in)

Miss Mya: (looking around with shock) Where is that troublesome learner?

Jackey: She went out right after you went to the principal's office.

Miss Mya: Fine. The class will be better off without her. Now, moving on. Wait a minute, why does it seem that Nashel and Vanessa are gone too?(suspicious)

Carrey: Obviously, they followed that self-centered...

Jackey: Carrey, stop.

Tofio: Miss, those girls don't actually know how life can be.

Miss Mya: Enough about them. When I came here I said we would learn about the STI's. Sadly something came up. You have to go home due to a meeting that all teachers must attend in 30 minutes. Now, off you go.

Scene 2

(in the street)
Vanessa: Girls, where are we off to?
Nashel: Yeah, where are you taking us, Babiecha?
Babiecha: Shut up and listen. We are rich. There is no need for us to stay in that stupid place.
Nashel: Good point.
Vanessa: You go, girl.
(walk away)

Scene 3

(Jackey, Tofio, Lung-star and Carrey chilling)
Jackey: Guys, do you think what Babiecha and her friends did was wise?
Tofio: My man, it was way out of line.
Carrey: They'll regret those actions.
Lung-star: Being rich is a blessing, but they don't seem to see it.
Jackey: Yeah hey, but what can we say? The choice is theirs.
Tofio: As they say, life is all about choices.
Carrey: But still, some choices are out of line.
Lung-star: Guys, it's getting late. Let's all go home.

Scene 4

(later that day Babiecha, Nashel and Vanessa in a shabeem drinking.)

Nashel: Babiecha, look at that guy. He's looking right at you.

Babiecha: Which one?

Nashel: (pointing) That one with the red jacket and a black jeans.

Babiecha: Yeah, don't act surprised. I'm hot and that's a fact. I bet he'll want to spend the night with me.

Vanessa: Go get him, tiger.

Babiecha: (walking away towards that man) See you later, alligators.

Friends: In a while, crocodile

EX: Hi little miss. I'm EX.

Babiecha: Hi, big buggy. I'm Babiecha.

EX: (whispers in her ear) Wanna get out of here and have some fun away from all these people?

Babiecha: What do you think? Lets get out of here.

(Babiecha runs out of the Shabeem with EX, her friends smiling, acting all happy for her)

Scene 5

(A week later Babiecha is sitting alone at her place)

Babiecha: (soliloquizing) What is (cough) wrong (cough) with me?
(Nashel and Vanessa arrive only to find their friend in a bad state of health)
Nashel: Hey, bad girl.
Babiecha: (cough) hey, (cough) hey, girls.
Vanessa: or not.
Nashel: What's wrong, babe?
Babiecha: (cough)
Vanessa: No look, she's coughing blood. Do your parents know about this?
Babiecha: No, and neither of you is going to tell them.
Nashel: If that's so, we're taking you to the Clinic.
Babiecha: But I'm fine.
Vanessa: Fine? Do you even know what that means? Just look at you.
(The girls walk to the clinic)

Scene 6

(At the clinic)

Nashel: Girl, you can go to the consulting room alone. We'll wait for you here.
Babiecha: Thanks, guys.
(She walks away)
Nashel: Vanessa, let's wait for her outside
(They walk outside)

Scene 7

(In the consulting room)
Nurse: Good day, young lady.
Babiecha: Good (cough) good day.
Nurse: Oh, my word! By the sound of that cough, I can tell you're not feeling well.
Babiecha: What could be wrong with me?
Nurse: First things first. Your name, please.
Babiecha: Babiecha Mpungi.
Nurse: (writing) Age?
Babiecha: 15.
Nurse: Open your mouth wide and let me put this object under your tongue.
(She puts a thermometer in Babiecha's mouth. After a minute she takes it out)
Nurse: Young girl, I'm going to have to do an H.I.V test.
(she does the test)
(looking straight on Babiecha's face)
Nurse: My girl, you're H.I.V positive.
Babiecha: No, I can't be. I'm a daughter of one of the richest men in this country.
Nurse: H.I.V can affect anyone, including the president, but it's your choice to let it take you down or fight it. Come back after two days. We still have to do more tests to determine what A.R.V.'s are suitable for your stage.

Scene 8

(Babiecha walks out of the room)
Babiecha: (crying) Girls, this is bad. My father will kill me.
Nashel: What? What is it, Babies?
Babiecha: I'm H.I.V. positive.
Vanessa: What! No, you can't be!
Nashel: No what?
Vanessa: Everything will be just fine. Let's take her home.

(they arrive at her place)

Nashel: Your dad is back, so we can't enter. See you later.
Vanessa: (walking the opposite direction after she had entered) Nashel, did you hear her? We must spread the word.
Nashel: Totally. Now that she's H.I.V. positive, we cannot be friends with her. We can't risk it.

Scene 9

(a morning in class)

Vanessa: (stands on the desk) Class, listen up.
Nashel: Babiecha, the drama queen of the class, is H.I.V positive.
(Babiecha enters the classroom and everyone runs away from her)
Babiecha: (crying as Miss Mya enters)
Miss Mya: What is going on here? Why is Babiecha crying?
Tofio: She's crying because she has H.I.V,
Vanessa: Yeah, she has AIDS.
Miss Mya: (takes a deep breath) No, learners. I see you are confused. Let me explain. First, H.I.V. and AIDS are two different things.
Carrey: How so?
Miss Mya: H.I.V. is a virus, whereas AIDS is a very critical stage of H.I.V. where you've got more than the H.I.V. alone in your system, e.g. you might be having T.B. together with H.I.V. Students, H.I.V. cannot be spread in the air. It can only spread through sexual activities and the contact with blood. You can never get it just by playing, hugging or even kissing someone who is infected. Babiecha, having the virus is not the end of the world. You can still live a normal life, just by taking care of yourself. And to all of you, you can still be friends with her. There is no harm in that.
Jackey: Wow, I didn't know that much.
Babiecha: Everyone, I'm so sorry for everything I've done in the past. I have learned my lesson the hard way. Let this be a lesson to all of us. Please forgive me, and do not make the same mistakes I made. I was just blinded by riches, but that is nothing now.
Lung-star: Never have I thought that this day would come.
Everyone: It's okay, Babies.

43

Babiecha: Thank you for another chance. I promise not to blow it.
(they all hug with joy)

Fly like the Eagle in You

Fly Like the Eagle in You

I was told about the failure I carry in my genes the person I was meant to be.
They determined who I was destined to be long before I even meditated on taking my first step.
A failure is what I was meant for in their eyes, a non-achiever is what they dreamt of me.
A mind cannot be read nor can a heart be studied.
They came in their millions to witness my failing in living.
They came with their smiles shining like the treasure the night skies carry though their hearts are as dark as a moonless night.
They came devoted to help dig a hole for my downfall.
It was now up to me to choose my own path.
At this time sophistication helped with no single way.
It was a choice I was to make sooner than later.
They chose a path for me leading to death, an internal death, a death that had no way back to life.
My inner person awoke to rise.
I came back to life like a super hero.
They did the worst on me but I did my best, my best to be seen, to be seen shining like the stars in the sky.
To be seen flying like a strong bird over the highest mountains over the highest skies like an Eagle, flying freely, ruling the skies, skies of my life.

I am flying like the EAGLE in me.

Who should I be?

Copyright © Jackey Mukhawana 2015

Who should I be?

How hard could it be to uncover?
Right before me
Except I can't seem to find the clear part of it.

Who am I meant to be?
Who am I to be?
All I know is that I'm an African,
Born in a free African Generation.

I try in a variety of ways to unfold my programmed mind
with an inaccessible password.
I try to be sophisticated, but end up abashed.

I try with all my strength to reach the top of the highest
African mountain, hoping to find the answer to my
seemingly complicated uncomplicated question.
I've looked everywhere in my surroundings, but no sign of it.

Hold on!! My heart; it holds the answer I seek.

Not found on the highest mountain nor under the deepest
oceans,
Just behind my chest, there it stands within my heart,
The key to acknowledging to myself who I am.

Who I am is a choice I alone have to build in my heart of
hearts.
Who I am is who I am.

Education

Education

A developer
A producer of dreams
A producer of a bright future
A great warrior that fights against poverty.

Oh education!
The healer of the pain caused by suffering.
Without you the youth of today have no future.

You are a true Icon.
Doctors, Engineers, Pilots...
You just name them.
They're all products of the producer education, named under
the beautiful blue sky.

Humans develop from the dark side of life, named before
suffering, poverty.

Indeed you are a fearless warrior that fights poverty strongly.

The key to success
The key to survival
The key to a brighter future.

Oh education!
The process of receiving or giving systematic instruction.

His name is Jesus

Copyright © Jackey Mukhawana 2015

His Name is Jesus

Wow!
Have you seen the power he carries.
So great that you can't explain
The light and happiness of his name.
He is the son of GOD.

His healing power is so awesome, amazing and oh
no need to mention Huge.
His name explains it all.
He has all the love no Human can give.

When his name is called, demons, demons tremble as though
they're cooked under the ultraviolet at its full range.

They run as though they see a volcano coming.

He is a man of kindness, love, care and so wise that he
always knows the way of truth.

His name is Jesus.

Electricity

Electricity

I am a force of power
So powerful that I make and destroy.
I'm not an invention, but a discovery.

I am of use to humans.
They use me happily, freely and carelessly.
They never meditate on how their lives would be if I
vanished.

It's so astonishing the way I am of help.
I'm no fire, but I burn.
I'm no car, but I move.
I'm no spice, but I garnish.
I am generated by a source of propulsion.

The more I'm used is the more I'm generated and the more
air is polluted.
I'm meant to light at night, but my ability to light is expanded
to day at noon.

I'm not a bird, but up in the sky, I'm there.
I'm a great legend of all times that no one ever appreciates.

I'm of help except I don't get a simple thank you.
Why me?
I'm used carelessly and obliviously.

From one household to another, I'm used throughout the day.

"Hikwalaho ka yini ndzi fanele ku twisiwa kuvava hindlela
leyi?"(why do I have to be hurt in this kind of way)
"Ndzi onhe yini mina?"(what wrong did I commit)
"Matirhiselo ya mina ya hundzisiwa mpimo"(my use has
become unlimited)

There's more demand than supply.
It's not because I'm not enough, but due to them using me
carelessly continuously.
Why does it have to be me?
Save me!
You, me, him, her, them, all of us
together as one can save electricity.
"xirilo xa gezi ixikulu swinene"(electricity's cry is very loud)

Oh! electricity

Together if we work as one and share our strength, ability,
knowledge and love for electricity, only then that what was
lost, will be again.

Electricity.

Ebola

Copyright © Jackey Mukhawana 2015

Ebola

A virus you are.
So heartless, merciless taking millions of lives every single
day
What wrong have we committed?
So many deaths of our brothers and sisters.

When will you ever stop?
Why do you have to be so heartless, careless in every way.
Painful not to be able to hug, kiss or even touch our friends,
families and heart abductors.

Where do you come from?
Which planet did you arrive from?
What kind are you?
Why are you so capable of killing this many?

Where do you get so much power?
Please stop. Too many deaths. It's enough.

Please. You have done enough damage.
We have felt the pain you've caused by taking our people.

Stop. It's enough. Stop taking so many lives.
We're on our knees as humans.
Please, Ebola, we've shed enough tears.

Enough is enough.
Please, Ebola,
Just let go, let go, Ebola.

Chain Breaker

Copyright © Jackey Mukhawana 2015

Chain Breaker

So strong
Stark in the family
Like a curse
A curse of all generations.

No one could break it,
binding every part of the clan and suppressing 'em to their
weakest points.

A genetic curse it was.
Unbroken, with its brightness as though it's of good.

A hero arose with massive strength,
A hero no one believed in.
Arisen to break this clan-chain.
Be strong and break it.

The past never determines the future.
Have a dream and polish it off with a vision.

With that, you have the greatest weapon of life.
Then, use it to break the chain,
The chain of suffering life.
Beside you, there stands education for a bright future.

Africa my mother land

Africa my Motherland

That is where my heart is set.
I may explore world-wide,
but there ain't no place like home.

Africa my love.
Africa my heart builder.
Full of culture and beings of "ubuntu".

Oh! Democracy is on our side.
Liberty rules,
Filled with love and joy.

Everyday filled with joy
and happiness shared within Africa.
Joyful like Christmas day.

The sun shines beautifully
for the great process of plants' life, photosynthesis
for better food, cleaner oxygen,
and beauty of nature.

They make fun of our skin colour.
It's a feature to be proud of.
Proud of the dark skin the father of humanity chose for us.

Full of beaches and greens,
The source of "ubuntu"

Africa, the source of all good.

Africa, my pride.
Africa, my love.
Africa, my heart.
Africa, the rhythm of my poem.
Africa, my home.

Africa, my motherland.
Africa, my fortress.

Bekazi Mboweni

Bekazi is a grade 9 student at Hudson Ntsan'wisi Senior Secondary School. She wrote the poem on "Electricity" that is also shown on my website.

She was born in Van Velden in Limpopo, South Africa. Bekazi has one sister and five brothers. She enjoys singing and writing. She believes that her calling in life is to become a Veterinarian.

Bekazi Mboweni

Electricity

Copyright © Bekazi Mboweni 2015

Electricity, electricity,
the power union of our lives,
the genius of lightness,
the supplement that makes
our lives easier in daily activities.
We salute you, electricity for how we are now.

Electricity the power.
Where do you come from?
Where does your power of lightness develop?
How does your name get so wide?
Your power, emotions and senses...

With my imagination I can follow your steps to reach
where the power
of your current might have been formed.
Everywhere we go there is electricity.
You're the best.
Go forward continuously all for the high support of your use.

Alter Mathebula

Alter Mathebula

Alter is in Grade 11 at Hudson Ntsan'wisi Senior Secondary School. She was born in Petanenge, the third of four children. Now age 16, she says she is a complete girl and in a complicated relationship. Alter is a story teller, a playwright and a poet.

The Magic Paint Brush

Not far away in a small village of Nkomanini, there once lived a well-known artist by the name of December who used the drip-drop technique and a paint brush to do his amazing work. One afternoon, he was walking near the river trying to picture in his mind something he could paint. Unexpectedly he heard a "vavavoom" voice. He listened very carefully while he was very scared, but he continued picturing. Again he heard "abracadabra" and he whispered "the magic word". He became more afraid.

Then it got worse. When he turned around, he was covered by a dark shade. He screamed loudly. "Noooo! What's going on here?" but nobody could hear him. He thought it was a curse.

After a while, he heard a loud voice. It said, "Don't be afraid. You have talent."

He stood tight and listened.

"Your uncle was an ESP. He had the ability to know something that will happen in the future or even what someone else is thinking. Now, close your eyes and imagine yourself in Halloween. Abracadabra."

December felt very sad.

"You can now open your eyes. Turn around and face the west."

December did as he was instructed by the voice.

He saw a beautiful paint brush, a mojo and alchemy (the magic powders).

"This is not just a paint brush but a magic paint brush. Take this as a gift from your great uncle. Mix the magic powders together and put the brush inside. Then whisper what you want to draw. Then it will do everything you instruct it to do."

December took the gift and went home. When he got home, he took out a painting board and his gifts and started to paint. He instructed the magic paint brush to paint a big boat. His interest in boats was a secret that he had never told anyone. He was amazed to see the paint brush doing its magic. It painted a very big beautiful boat. He continued using the paint brush to paint many things which he sold. Some he posted in his room.

One afternoon, he was painting a picture of a house nearer the road. There came four giant men and found him painting. They bullied him and threw away the picture he had painted. They broke his magic paint brush. December went home and couldn't eat that day.

While the men were walking away, they heard a voice commanding them: "Die because of your ungratefulness". Unbelievably, they all died.

December woke up the next morning and found a box with magic powders and a paint brush. He heard a voice say "The white magic will never disappoint you."

He was happy ever after.

Consequences of a Friendship

Copyright © Alter Mathebula 2015

It was awful. Although she was surprised to see him, she had no idea she was in danger. The whole thing took her by surprise. Just because she saw them, she got in trouble. Maybe, if she had told her friend what she had seen, it would have been better.

Her friend knew nothing about it and she still doesn't know. The only thing that was running in her mind was "NOTHING BUT THE TRUTH". Just because she is her friend, he thinks that she has told her. Like the reality speaks of the angels.

It was Wednesday morning. She was about to write an English test on the 13th day of May 2015. He got into her class. There were about 31 learners in the room. He was rolling eyes looking around. She was not aware that he was looking for her.

Then, there at the first desk from the door near the window, there she was. He saw her. He was not alone, but with his friend. By then, many questions started competing in her mind. Their answers were acting hard to get, but shamelessly he started doing his will.

Without asking, he started what he came for. He started beating her. I can still hear the voices of her classmates. It was very awkward.

Just before she left the classroom, everyone was busy asking why he is doing this. But unfortunately, he was the only person who knew the answer.

She thought maybe it's because he once fell for her and she was not interested, but only to find out later that that she was. It was that awkward moment when you are beaten for no reason, just for the consequences of a friendship

After leaving the classroom, remember it was at school and everyone was watching, she went to the staff room to report, only to find out that the teachers were in a SADTU meeting.

She was afraid. What if he comes back and beats her again? It was very painful, but interesting at the same time. After a few minutes, the meeting was over and she ran to her class teacher to ask for assistance.

This beating happened about half an hour before she should start with her English test. Her teacher just said to her "My child, get back to your class now and write the test. We will discuss this later."

He was never penalized. They didn't even discuss the matter with him. The case was dropped in that way from then on.

Hours passed by and finally she let everything go. She didn't believe in a friendship again. From then on, she knew the consequences of that kind of friendship.

My life, my journey

My name is Ofentse. I am a 16-year-old teen, an A student and a hard worker. I am my own hero and I never lose hope or ever give up.

I always dedicate myself in anything I do. My short term goal is to pass grade 12. Medium term goal is to go to university, study actuarial sciences and get a job. My long term goal is to find December still waiting for me so we can build up a family together.

My father passed away on the 15th of September, 2012. I was doing grade 8 and it was my first year in high school.

My mother is a caring mom; she provides for my sisters and me, though she chooses sides between my sisters and me sometimes.

My father was the only person I was very close to in my family. Since he passed away, I started being lonely. Life started to go hard from then. I just thank God because I still have my mom.

I am a lonely girl, but the interesting thing is that my boyfriend is my adviser.

I am in a relationship with December Malatji, a 20-year-old guy. I am happy to be with him even though people say he is older than I. What I know is that age is just a number.

December and I started dating on the 13th of February 2013 . It all started as a joke and ended up as a relationship. I always sacrifice my time to please him because he cares .Though people think I am foolish, because he was well-known as a playboy, the reality is that people change.

He always reminds me to read my books every minute. It is hard to find such a guy in life.

Since I met him, things started to change in my life. He made me feel appreciated. The loneliness faded away, but because he had to leave me and focus on his studies, he left me behind. This didn't change anything because he continued calling and checking if I was still fine.

He made me realize that not all people will love or like me, but he does.

One very boring day while I was at school, I was sitting alone in class when I heard Colin talking about Jackey.

I knew Jackey long before, but we were not friends. Colin was talking about Jackey's new book "My Life, My Misery".

He made me realize that there was something I also had to do. I knew that I also love writing. During break time, I went to grade 10A to look for Jackey.

Jackey is a very friendly guy. He made me laugh even though I was bored. Jackey immediately saw that I was lonely. He asked to be my friend before I got to business and I confirmed his request.

Now I was free to talk to my new friend. I started asking him about his book. He gave me useful details. Then I told him I also felt lonely only when boredom strikes.

Jackey was different from many people I met. Thank God I finally have someone to talk to. Jackey and I became good friends from that day on. He treats me with care and shows respect. I took him as a brother and I was a sister to him. Because Jackey has other friends, he has to spend much time with them rather than with me.

Though I needed someone who is also lonely to cheer me up, Jackey introduced me to his publisher, William Jenkins. I found William to be friendly, just like Jackey. Then I started writing a family saga. Every time I write how I feel, it makes me feel better than telling somebody else.

This was not bad, but I still felt lonely. December and Jackey are the people I have in my life. They always support and encourage me in every situation. They make me not worry or ever give up. They play a big role in my life.

Though I feel lonely sometimes, I know I have people to run to. I thank God because he gave me December, a good boyfriend, and Jackey as my good friend also. They are the reason why I never give up.

Never give up

Copyright © Alter Mathebula 2015

Thandeka is a 16-year-old girl. She lives in a small village of Gabaza. She is currently doing grade 11. Thandeka is an author and she does not have a friend at school.

Having a friend is not a priority, but being a good advisor is a good decision. My mates always made fun of me, but I never gave up. It was not an easy pathway to walk through but I finally made something out of nothing.

In life, all you need is to know who you are and what you need, then you will succeed. I always consider myself as a crayon. I may not be your favourite color, but one day you will need me to complete a picture.

One morning after the school holidays, I got into my class and my mates were there . They were sitting in groups as they always do. I had no friend and I felt very lonely. They started laughing at me and I ignored them, but with a broken heart. Sometimes keeping quiet can be the best solution. I went and took a seat and started writing. I really knew that better days were coming.

My mother always told me that, "do what pleases you and forget about what people think". She always told me to be my own self and live life my own way. Every time people started making funny faces, I would just turn and show them my back.

I always stayed alone during breaks and also in class. It was very bad because I had no one to talk to. What I did made me realize something that many people have never understood. A brighter future is for the hard workers who never give up.

Out of my classmates, nobody loved me. I didn't need them to, so it was fine with me and it had to do for them also. What was hard was that they had a verbal war with me.

Teenage stage was really a big problem that introduced itself in my life. I almost felt like dropping out of school and giving up; then I thought of my background. I knew that my family was counting on me, haters were looking at me and my community was putting their trust in me.

I didn't want to disappoint people who care and love me. My mother always gave me support and encouraged me. My pastor at church always preached of a message that was really directly speaking to my life.

I needed to make a real change, a big change to people out there, people who gave up because they had no friends, people who dropped out of school because mates were making fun of them

If you know what's best for you, then go for it. Never give your enemies a chance to bring you down. Do not cry in front of them. All you have to do is to sit back and say "God bless them" and show them sympathy, because they don't know what they are doing.

Never lose hope. Never give up. Try your level best and do what's best for you

The Journey I Walked Through

Copyright © Alter Mathebula 2015

Characters

Tinyiko Mathebula, Crate packer at Hippo steel suppliers at Tzaneen, where he has been working for about 8 years.

Dorries Mathebula, Tinyiko's wife. They have been married for almost 22 years. Now, she doesn't have a job.

Joy Mathebula. Their only child who is almost 17 years of age.

Scene 1

This family of three live in a simple 5-roomed house in a village called Petanenge. Their house was built in the 90's. It is divided into a kitchen, 3 bedrooms and a living room.

(It is Saturday morning. Tinyiko is in his bedroom preparing for work.)

Tinyiko: (thinking to himself) Just as always, trying my best to look after my family, but no! I always fail. Even when I was young, my mother always told me that life is like a journey, you enjoy the ride or suffer non-stop.

(Joy rushes into the room, carrying a bucket of water)

Joy: Daddy, are you going to work today?

Tinyiko: Yes, Princess. It is my responsibility.

(asking questions as though he doesn't want any answers)
What will you eat if I don't go to work?
Where will you get money for school fees?
Who is going to take care of you?

Joy: Oh daddy, you are a real man. You know, it's a great pleasure for me to have a great dad like you.

Tinyiko: Princess, your grandmother always told me that a real man is one who suffers to give the best to his family.

Joy: And that's what you are doing. I'm so proud of you daddy.
(rolling her eyes filled with tears)
What you do is enough for me.

Tinyiko: Thank you, my Angel. Know that I will always try my best to do what's best for you and your mother.
(checking the time)
Oh my God! Time is flying like crazy.
(rushing to carry his briefcase)
See you later, Princess.

Joy: Bye, daddy. Take care.

Scene 2

(Joy rushes to the kitchen and finds her mother washing the dishes)

Joy: May I help you with the dishes, Mom?

Dorries: Yes, baby girl, and oh, when we finish, I'd like to talk to you about something, but for now, let's scrub these pots.

(after washing the dishes they go to the sitting room and have their talk)

Dorries: You know my child, your father is trying by all means to make money, but I'm worried that you'll have to spend almost two years at home after matriculating before he can make enough money for you to go to university.

Joy: Mommy, that's just another part of this misery, and yes, I understand that we don't have enough money, so I'll wait.

Dorries: Thank you for understanding, sweety. You can see that we eat the same meal almost every day. Just be strong and believe that one day is one day. God will make a way.

Joy: Amen

(Tinyiko comes back home feeling pains all over his body)

Tinyiko: (with a small voice) Good day, family.

Both mother and daughter: Good day, Daddy.

Joy: Daddy, how was your day at work?

Tinyiko: Same as always, Angel. Working hard every day to stay alive.

Dorries: (shakes her head out of sadness)

Tinyiko: Today was just one of those days and I'm feeling very tired and my body is paining badly.

Dorries: Oh no, hubby, but worry not. I know just what to do to get rid of the pains.
(turning to Joy)
Baby girl, please go to the kitchen and boil some water for your father.

Joy: Okay Mom. (running to the kitchen to do as she's told)

(Dorries help her husband to the bedroom and they start talking in the bedroom)

Tinyiko: Dorries

Dorries: Yes, my love.

Tinyiko: Come sit beside me. I want to talk to you about something important.

Dorries: (serious face) What is it, Tinyiko?(sitting next to her husband on the bed)

Tinyiko: My wife, please never lose hope. As you can see, I'm not feeling well. I could die at any time.

Dorries: Come on, Tinyiko, you're just tired and no one has ever died because of being tired. (smiling)

Tinyiko: You don't understand. I am suffering from Pneumono Ultramicroscopicsilico Valcanoconiosis, and my lungs are getting weaker minute by minute.

Dorries: No Tinyiko. You can't die. How am I supposed to take care of Joy? I don't have a job. There are so many questions piling in my mind. Please my love, never leave me. Why didn't you tell me earlier?(crying)

Tinyiko: I didn't want you to worry. Please take care of Joy. It seems my journey ends here.

Dorries: No. I refuse to accept it. (crying)

Tinyiko: Please call Joy for me.

Dorries: (whiping her tears) Joy! (loudly) Joy!

Joy: Yes, mother. (running to their bedroom)

Tinyiko: My angel come and sit next to daddy. (Joy moves and sits there)
My princess, daddy is not feeling well. I'm suffering from a lung disease and it's at the last stage, meaning that I can join the ancestors at anytime.

Joy: Daddy, please tell me I'm dreaming. You can't leave us, you can't die. You just can't. (crying)

Tinyiko: Princess, it's out of my hands. Please do this one thing for me. Remember to say something good to yourself every day. When you make mistakes, always try your best to find a way to fix them. Learn to forgive people and not to

hold grudges. Joy, be strong. Take care of your mother for me. Family, I love you and I
(he stops talking, and a second later he stops breathing. Mother and daughter cry like crazy).

Scene 3

(It's the 1st of September, 2012. It's Tinyiko's funeral at Petanenge village. Family and friends have assembled at the graveyard to say their farewells to Tinyiko.)
(Pastor Mkhari sharing the word of God at the graveyard)

Pastor Mkhari: Remember that Jesus said "My soul will now leave your body forever, but you will live with me forever." The bible says "earth to earth, ashes to ashes and dust to dust" so we honour the Lord our God and we say to the family and friends, May Tinyiko Mathebula's soul rest in peace.

Joy: (crying very loudly from a distance away from the grave) I will always remember you every single day of my life, but because God did this for his reasons, I will.
(she pauses and cries very loudly as her family tries to stop her from crying)

Dorries: (crying silently) Rest in peace, my husband. I thank God for he knows and he does. May he protect your soul. Amen

(Everyone goes their separate ways)

Success

Not far away from books,
It's like the dry river beds
crying and seeking water.
Not just a petite word,
But too robust to take responsibilities.
The way of light,
The key to brightness,
The family of all kinds,
The wish everyone has,
The magic to succeed.

Success!

You are the solution to our everyday problems.
You are the giver of brighter future,
The developer of doctors, presidents and scientists,
You have the white magic,
The right way to make life easier.

What is life?

Copyright © Alter Mathebula 2015

They say it's a journey.
Then, they define it as from B to D,
From birth to death.
But what's between B and D?
It's a C.
So what is "C"?
It's a choice.
Isn't meant to be easy,
It's meant to be lived.
Sometimes good, other times rough,
But with all the ups and downs
You learn lessons that make you stronger.
Our life is a matter of choices.
Live well and it will never go wrong.
One most appreciated precious thing:
Life!
The journey defined as from B to D.

Books

Defined as papers punched together with a hard cover,
Well known as printed with black ink,
But what is the role of the ink?
Not to be thrown away,
Even packed angelic at the library;
But to be read
Not just printed,
But to give away useful information
To make our minds massive,
Develop our knowledge further,
Bring skills to our new world,
Reduce stress to our daily living,
Share the joy of the world,
To acknowledge us of the secret,
The secret of success.
That secret of humanity,
They give the power to stand and lead the world.
Books: we salute you.

Drug

Copyright © Alter Mathebula 2015

I am a drug, a monster that can never be destroyed.
I am a destroyer of your mind.
I can take you from low to high, then I make you fall to zero.

Once you start committing yourself to me, it's hard to take
me out of your life.
Once I get into your mind, all I do is destroy your thinking.

When you're introduced to me, I will make you feel bossy.
Once I start getting your attention, you will never recognize
yourself again.

I came to steal, to kill and to destroy.
Once I start having control over you, you will regret it for the
rest of your life.

You better STOP using me, because I'm dangerous.
I am always like a hungry Python.
Once I grab you, they will never get you back.

BEWARE! and STOP using me or you will suffer the
consequences.

Be yourself

Sit back and listen.
I never gave up.
Inside a troubled soul you cannot find love, joy or peace.

They always talk and it hurts.
Open your eyes and close your ears.
Just let them talk.

No friends?
Always say to yourself, "I was born alone".
Never lose hope.
Go ahead and be yourself.
Put aside trouble, hatred, and fear.
Just find your way.

Let them say you're not worth it, but tell yourself you can
have it.
Just be yourself.
When they walk away from you, let them walk.

Never let your enemies trouble you.
Standup and say "you're wasting your time".
Show them humanity.
They will be ashamed and just carry on.
Be yourself.

Don't be afraid.
Walk with pride and do your best.
Let them suffer the consequences of hatred and be your own
hero.

I am wise enough

Copyright © Alter Mathebula 2015

I may not know you better, but I am wise enough;
I am wise enough to know my inner self.
I may not know the truth, but I can tell that you are lying.
I may not be perfect, but I am wise enough,
Wise enough to accept the way I am.
I am wise enough, wise enough to humble myself before God.

I may not know him by flesh, but I am wise enough to communicate with him.
I may not be able to read, write or to sing,
But I am wise enough to raise my voice.

Wise enough to hear and obey his word.
I am wise enough, wise enough to differentiate between good and bad.
I am wise enough to see through you.

I may not be rich, but I am worth it.
I may not look better than you, but I am wise enough to do better than you can.

I may not know the cure for H.I.V. and AIDS,
But I am wise enough to know that it kills,
Wise enough to define my name.
I am wise enough to choose good over bad.
I am wise enough to take a step forward.
I may not know how to define love, but I am wise enough,
Wise enough to know how to love.
I am wise enough to prevent hurt by laughter,
I am wise enough!

That time will arrive

Copyright © Alter Mathebula 2015

Sit back and listen.
The truth hurts.
Poetry in motion.

They always talked, talked and talked, but I never listened.
They told me the time will arrive, the time when you will cry
alone, the time when you will remember the words of people
who gave advice

That time will arrive.

The time you will think of days back then,
Back when you used to fool yourself.
Time when you recognize you were blinded.
When you will cry to go back and fix your mistakes.

That time will arrive.

The time when you will realise you used to play not pay.
When you threw your future away.
The time when you will realise the truth.

That time will arrive.

The time when you will have to take care of a baby, when
you can't even take care of yourself.
The time when you will have to think of someone else and
forget all about yourself.

That time will arrive.

Boyfriend

You ruined my life.
You played my heart like a toy.
You made me a fool, so you embarrassed me.
Indeed, you are a destroyer.

I gave you everything.
You lied to me and made me go blind.

Okay, I was blinded by love.
You stole my heart and trust.
I am to trust no one anymore.
You're a perfect liar.

You took my Virginity away.
You left me with a baby, then you ran away.
You said I was your first priority.
Now where are you to prove your points?

You have forsaken me in the middle of nowhere.
You turned around and showed your back.

I dropped out of school because of you.
I hate you now. You made me feel worthless.
My love is now price-tagged, just because of you.

My reputation is ruined.
It's all about YOU, YOU, YOU.
Damn a boyfriend! What is that? Food?

NO!A boyfriend is a destroyer and a perfect liar.

To Mom

Copyright © Alter Mathebula 2016

With ups and downs, with or without food or money,
Without shelter nor water to drink,
You raised me up.

Nine months in full you carried me.

You are my friend, my smile keeper, my adviser and my pain
killer.
Words from your mouth are adorable.

Ndzi khensa rirhandzu ra wena manana.
(I am thankful for your love).

My heart belongs to you.
You carried me for nine months in full.
You have never forsaken me.
I am here because of you.

Abortion clinics were there, the choice was yours.
Thanks; you decided to keep me.
You bent but never broke.
You raised me up to more than I can be.

u xiluva xa mbilu Yanga .Ndzi nga va yini xana handle ka
wena?.
Rirhandzu ra wena ri ndlandlamuke ku tlurisa malwandle

You are the flower, the rose of my heart.
Who can I be without you?
Indeed your love is wider than oceans.
You are everything I need.

Poetry

Copyright © Alter Mathebula 2016

My name is poetry.
I don't really know my surname.
I am commonly used by poets.
They bring peace to shattered hearts through me.

I can hurt you.
I am capable of making you cry or laugh.
I can break and repair your heart at the same time.

I have that strength.
Whenever you are down, I can raise you up.
If your spirit is low, I can cheer you up.
I'm capable of bringing joy to families.

Ask William Shakespeare and Delmira Agustini.
They will tell you.

I showed them the spirit in me.

poetry♥

The secret heart

Copyright © Alter Mathebula 2016

Half in my dreams somebody knocked.
I was afraid to open the doors of my heart,
Woke up in the morning trying to figure out who he was.
Unfortunately, I cannot make a prophecy.

Again, someone knocked.
Then I opened the door for this somebody.
There was my secret admirer,
Somebody special, someone different.
I called out his name "DESMOND".

In my heart, he belongs.
His picture is always in my eyes.
My heart trembles whenever I hear his voice.

My smile keeper, my pain killer, my friend and my best
companion,
Surely our love grows wider than oceans every second of the
day.

Oh my! The secret heart.♥

First Love

Copyright © Alter Mathebula 2016

Remember the first day we met?
Our first touch?
Remember our first kiss?
The first time we hugged?
All the good memories we left behind?

That was our first love.

When I looked down, afraid to look at you, straight into your eyes,
And you would ask "uni chava yini?",
A question I have never answered.

That was our first love.

It was beautiful how it grew every second of the day.

Uthando♥ Love♥ Rirhandzu.

Death

Copyright © Alter Mathebula 2016

There's no mercy in you.
You separate us from our loved ones,
You leave us with broken hearts.
Rifu una Mona.

You don't even bother to knock.
What you do is come in without permission.

Your power took our great grandmothers (Gogomu).
Once you take, you never bring back.

Trying to fight you is a battle we will never win;
That's what we realized,
So we surrender to you.
xikombelo xinwe ntsena eka wena,
Stay away from us.

H.I.V. and A.I.D.S

Copyright © Alter Mathebula 2016

A virus you are.
You killed our sisters and brothers.
You make our grandmothers and grandfathers suffer.

U xihlamariso ha Kunene.

Four years back, you took my father.
Now, my mother is suffering from you.
Why aren't you ashamed?
Where do you come from?
I bet your parents might be witches.

You are a killer, not a destroyer.
Laha u nghenaka kona wa hlasela.

Let our poor Nation survive.
You have caused enough damage.

H.I.V. and A.I.D.S.,
Have mercy and return to your parents.

Eustacia Ntsakisi Nhlangweni

Eustacia Ntsakisi Nhlangweni

Here are two more recent photos of Eustacia.

Eustacia Ntsakisi Nhlangweni

Eustacia was born on the 28th of February, 2000. She lives at Dan village (Rhulani), Limpopo Province, South Africa. She is the only child of Calfonia Mashudu Mamafha and the first child of Tiyani Sambo.

She has three aunts: Akani, Phindile and Selina. She lives with her Grandmother.

She started her primary education at Banana primary school and also went to Ritavi primary school. She is in Grade 10 at Hudson Ntsan'wisi Senior Secondary school in the science stream.

At Banana primary school, a teacher helped her to continue with poetry. She started to express her feelings by writing poems and also wrote a story about her life.

She has an amazing friend, Jackey Mukhawana, who encourages her to continue writing. Her dream has always been to see her poems out there in the world.

She is a kind girl who likes playing with everyone. She wants to put herself at the same level as others and likes making new friends.

The Story of my Life

Copyright © Eustacia Ntsakisi Nhlangweni 2015

"Turning and turning in a widening gyre"[1], not knowing
where to go nor where to look for my beloved family, it
seems the world is turning against me or the other way
around.
I cannot hear the falconers, nor the falcons.

My world is falling apart.
The centre cannot hold.
Full of passionate intensity; surely I know that is my story.
Some revelation is at hand.
My story forsakes people and runs away with me.

At some point, my hair rises, eyes dilate and hands can grasp
no more.
My mind is one thing I lost.
I know that something queer is happening.
Suddenly, I have "miles to go before I sleep"[2].

The widening gyre is turning into rage at me.
I hear angry voices.
Something different is about to happen and I feel weak and
unprepared.

---

[1] William Butler Yeats The Second Coming 1919
[2] Robert Frost Stopping by Woods on a Snowy Evening 1922

A Fool

A fool I was thinking you were the best for me.
A fool I was thinking that you truly loved me.
A fool I was to believe you when you said you loved me
dearly.

Above all, I was a fool because I believed you when you said
you'd never cheat.
I hope we weren't meant to be together because you fooled
me saying that we were made to love.
I was a fool to fall for your stupid tricks.

Amongst all, I was a fool in a widening gyre of people
laughing at me as though I was finished.

Even the girls with whom you cheated stand in the
background to join in.
They laugh forgetting that tomorrow awaits them.
Now I am a fool no more, but you all are.

All my fears, my tears, my worries, have passed on.
All those who laughed made me strong.
I live every day of my life pitying you.

My Everything

I gave you everything.
What you took from me was my pride, my joy, my dignity,
my happiness.
You took more than I could give.

When you were lost and unable to recognize yourself, I was
there to help you find your inner you.
In spite of what I've done for you, you went out and spread
lies about me.
I was there when you really wanted me to be there.
I gave you all that I could afford, mostly my unconditional
love.
You took it all away and now I feel that my love is price-
tagged.
Love really blinded me.

For My Mother

So elegant, brave, strong, but sometimes hard to understand.
My crystal, my better half.
You always have a way of making me happy when I'm sad.
People might sometimes look at me and see a mistake, but
you never see me as one.

You never listen to what people say about me...because you
believe that I'm a child of God.
I couldn't have asked for a better mother.
You bring out the best in me.

I have gone miles to find words to show my gratitude, but
what amazes me is that no words can ever express my love
for you.
You are the reason I stand still when I shake.

My Testimony

Copyright © Eustacia Ntsakisi Nhlangweni 2015

Started off as an ordinary child, a child who people looked at
and saw as a mistake.
Many had criticized, teased, taken advantage of me, but still
those criticisms made me grow stronger and wiser.

Thought of giving up.
God made me grasp people to follow their lead, but it turned
out to be the wrong lead.
Tried to hide my feelings and cry inside.
That caused a disease.
A little voice inside was tellin' me to keep on climbing.
I can surely make it. God made me.

I've seen people fall. I chose to rise and show the inner me.
I've been told to sit down, but I decided to be a-climbin' on.
Taken all the phobia out of being in the dark, but the Most
High put me in the light.

Struggling to make friends in my childhood years all because
of where I come from.
Tears filled my eyes all night asking my purpose.
To me it seemed I had none.

Back then, I didn't get the chance.
The words that spelled "you", I mean "you", were never
there.
Now I've told myself that even though I didn't get the chance
then, now I have the chance and time to fulfill my dreams,
the dreams I didn't have when I was young.
Time to pick up the joy I didn't have.
Time to be who I want to be.

94

Poetry

My oh my!
I am that thing many of you use to express your feelings.
That thing that knows a lot of your secrets...Oh my!

I'm used to hurt others and it's good for me.
I'm used to make people happy and it's good for me.
I'm used in ways of reconciliation and it's still good for me.
I'm used to help others, yet it does me good.
I make people fall in love.
That does me greater good than Good...Oh my!

I'm good and evil and yet you never get to see my evil side.
You take all your deepest secrets and place them unto me.
All your fears, you put them in writing.
All in the name of my poetic self...My oh my!

The rhythm, the simile, the metaphor,
The personification, the alliteration,
The oxymoron, the onomatopoeia,
And emos are all placed upon this small poetic self.

Poetry is my name.
I'm for many who write and recite poems.
Little do many know of Me...
I'm the language of a few, but many like me.
I'm adored by a few, but many want to listen to me through
others who adore me...
I'm felt by a few, but many want to be felt by people who
write me...My oh my!

Friend

Copyright © Eustacia Ntsakisi Nhlangweni 2015

A comforter, a shoulder to cry on, a pillar of strength, an adviser, an ear to listen, a heart to feel, a smile keeper, a painkiller... All these are put to one thing that is a FRIEND.

We might go through thick and thin, but our friendship remains.

Others want to talk, but our ears always have lids to put on when negativity bursts from their mouths.

Anyone can be a friend, but only one can be a true friend who sticks around even when times are bad, who protects us from cat fights, who protects us from arguments, who advises us at all times.

We might fight as we can't always walk on crystals.
There are also stacks in the way.
We forgive one another as we know our friendship is rare.
They try to make us repel.
Fortunately enough, we are made stronger.
That helps us attract each other even more.

My back, my other half, my eyes, my heart, my hands, my legs, through good times you're always beside me.
You know what it takes to make me smile and frown.
You lead me not astray, but in the right path.
A friend you are, a friend you'll always be.
A friend no one has ever seen, a friend only I have had,
Kind to all, but different to me.

Dance with Daddy

For that moment I missed, for the chance I never had,
For the times we never had,
I remembered that we owed each other a dance...

Many steps I missed starting from the toddling stage to the
first step I took.
The first word I said was supposed to go with a dance.
A dance of excitement...
A dance of celebration...
A dance of achievements to be made in the future...
For the chance I did not have…

But all that remains are the thoughts,
Thoughts of how much fun it could have been,
Thoughts of the mark it would have left...
Thoughts of the great memories of our special dance.

Hopes for the few dances left.
A dance of teenhood,
To the dance of high school,
To university level,
To the first day at work.

Hoping for those dances,
Wishing for special time,
A special moment,
A fortunate chance,
All by grace,
For a dance with you.

Teen Life

Said to be the most difficult stage, but I say that I haven't
seen the difficulties of this age group.
All is the same to me.
All counts to your behaviour.
All counts to what you believe in.
All counts to what you're aiming for.

Wherever you go you hear people saying that 'peer pressure'
defines the difficulties perfectly.
Who said all teens live their lives to satisfy teens?
Who said all teens carry negativity?
Who said peer pressure has more power than your heart?
Who said peer pressure is only for teens?

From what I've heard, we all have a right to say what we
believe in, to talk our hearts and minds out, to show the
world what we are made of.

Teen stage is not a stage of difficulties, but a stage of getting
enough time to mature, enough time to learn responsibilities,
a chance to figure our plans, our dreams, our futures.

It is the foundation of adulthood.

Friendship

We met by chance and we became friends by choice.
Friendship is a strange thing.
A friend, a lover, an ear to listen, a heart to feel, and no
matter what happens, I call you friend.

We may argue, but we care because we are friends.
Our friendship has no beginning or end.
I fell in love with the idea of being your friend.
You smiled back at me.
I'm so blessed to have you as a friend.

New Generation

This generation was supposed to bring good things along
with it, but it brought the exact opposite.
Fathers no longer protect their children, but abuse them.
Doctors don't heal patients, but they sexually abuse them.

Young girls never take time to sit down, study, and plan their
future.
They roam around the streets turning themselves into
prostitutes or baby makers.

Police officers don't arrest suspects, but work hand-in-hand
with them.
The leaders of our country are corrupt, making the economy
fall, instead of growing it.

Heart (Love).

Last morning the deepest feeling of love knocked at my door
and I asked who it was.
The love said:
For the past years, months, weeks, days, hours, minutes,
seconds, you were waiting for your heart to be inculcated
with a deep heart.

Philosopher of pain knocked the stars down to fall and rise,
To give distaste and ambivalence to my heart and rise
against the mountain of love.

For I gave you the best I can and I can't pretend, because
your voice is full of love.
One tear of a bird unwrapped my tears and filled my eyes
with a simple flower.

Lost in the losing world, sorry times are no more hard.
I don't even know how to be sad or blue.
Love in excellence, friendship for life, magic personified.
Innocent thirsty emotions will buy every taste of joy and
dreams.

My Country

A wind is ruffling the tawny pelt of my country.
Only the birds cry 'Waste no compassion on these separate Dead'.

The green smell of burnt palm trees; in the sky, the reflections of fire.
The burning coal consuming with fire the warm country of the horizons, sleepless women thinking to buy plates to eat on.

Batten upon the bloodstreams of the veldt from the parched river on beast-teeming plain, corpses are scattered through a paradise.
The result of colonial policy to savages expendable as Jews?
Like natural law...

Men seek their divinity by inflicting pain.

Culture

Between me and you it's a vast sea.
Language and culture are not the same.
So very little I know of your history,
But I'm so crazy about the way you are.

We're an ocean apart, a mile away,
Yet I feel you paint from a distance.
Somehow, I see clearly.
Oh, I'm so crazy about the way you are.

Yeah, I'm so crazy I have to sing
The song in my heart: awe and wonder.
Love is incredible, rush amazing, thunder.
I'm crazy about you.
You're the reason I am who I am.

So grateful to you.
The colors you give me are wonderful.
Culture, oh culture, my best describer.

Praise God in Style

Copyright © Eustacia Ntsakisi Nhlangweni 2015

See, with God, you will sing. Almost is never enough.
Be like Ariana Grande and he will be your everything.
If you stick with him, you will upgrade from being a sinner
to a saint.
All you gotta do is put his name on your tattooed heart...

And if the devil asks 'waka bani ke lo!?'
Tell him 'ngi waku Jesu osindisayo impilo za Bantu'...

Like Coco Jones, enter his holy house with reverence
And when the Devil claims to know your future,
Tell him Mister, who I'm gonna be isn't up to you,
It's up to me.

Tell God that...
Yeah, it's you, the one I wanna spend my life with.
You don't have to own rands and nairas
To have him by your side.
You just have to worship him.

Don't let the fire burn, but keep the sparkle between you and
God...
Join Fifi Cooper and tell the Devil 'Gore a chechele
morago'.
Love him like your gonna lose him.

Guess I have to let people know that
'zange ndifumane omunye ondi khathalela njengaye yenu
Phethe impilo yami'.
Oh, Jesu, Jesu, Jesu!!!
Cry to God and he will make a way for you.

Fake Love

You meet a girl...wow!
Okay, you become friends with her...
Great, right?
You share secrets with her...
She's a friend material, hey!
You make her angry...
She cries and comes back to apologize even though you're
the one who wronged her.

She's one of a kind.
Don't you think so, too?
She shares her problems with you; you comfort her.
It was all going well, right?
A year passed. You must be really good friends...

During the second year, she confesses her feelings.
You play along...
She makes sacrifices to see you; you pretend to care.
She opens her legs for you.
You enjoy every moment.
Tomorrow comes, you cut her off..

She gets stressed.
She prays, she regrets, she tries to kill herself.
You come to her and tell her that you've got problems
Only to find out that you're going
To say that your chick broke up with you.

That's fake love, dude.
Better follow the person who loves you for who you are,
A person who cares.

Mistakes

Mistakes happen, and we learn from those mistakes...
Following thy heart may lead to many mistakes.
Sacrifices may lead to mistakes,
Young love can lead to bigger mistakes.

You may be promised heaven and earth, but they never tell
you what's at risk.
They buy you expensive stuff that makes you forget what's at
stake.
Remember! Mistakes happen everywhere, every hour, every
minute, every day.
You never know.

Nothing hurts more than knowing that you're a mistake.
Parents may not tell you,
Relatives may not tell you.
The people around you may stay out of it, but whenever they
talk about the past, it's gonna make you think twice.

That moment may make you feel not wanted.
It may make you think only about negatives in your life.
Thinking that you don't have a purpose,
Wanting to commit suicide,
But the little voice in you tells you something else.

Being a mistake doesn't mean that you should not behave
like a normal kid.
You are normal, you are unique, you are human and you
deserve equal treatment.
Don't look down on yourself.
Try to avoid the same mistakes your folks made.

How do you?

Copyright © Eustacia Ntsakisi Nhlangweni 2015

How do you claim that your gonna love someone like your
gonna lose them, and yet make them feel neglected?
You'll never know what people want.

How do you go around claiming that you're the best adviser
whilst you go around tellin people that they should follow
their hearts and take their minds with them?
Do hearts speak? Do hearts think?
Does your mind have legs to walk?
Does your mind have knees to crawl?
Does your mind have wings to fly?

The answer to that is NO!!
You cannot speak without a mouth.
Hearts don't have mouths.
Minds don't have legs or wings.

Don't say you will love a person 'til the end of time whilst
you know that come sunshine you will leave that person.
Don't promise girls trains and forget railways.
Don't promise them heaven and earth when you cannot reach
both worlds.

Unpredictable life

You never know what your gonna feel.
Neither can you predict when the feeling is gonna end.
It vanishes just like that, unexpectedly.
Things just change when you don't expect them to.
Nobody knows what the future has in store for us.

One minute you think that you have the world at your
shoulders, but in reality, the world has you.
Life is so unpredictable.
You might see a person today and get to hear about his death
tomorrow.

Death doesn't have a friend.
In the morning you find that the world is full of happy faces.
Come night, you find that all the happy faces have changed
to being drear faces.
Everything that has to do with life is unpredictable.
Tomorrow turns out to be a mystery.

About the Publisher

Mr. William Jenkins was born in Ottawa in 1932. After completing a degree in Mathematics and Physics at Queen's University at Kingston in 1954, he became a computer programmer and worked in that field for 45 years. Subsequently, he sold residential real estate and then wrote and published a few stories for middle-school children.

He is especially interested in publishing stories and poems from students. So far, only a few students from South Africa have submitted their writing.

If you are a teacher or student, submit creative writing as an email attachment to

williamhenryjenkins@gmail.com.

There is no charge for services. The only out of pocket cost to Mr. Jenkins for this hobby is the cost of printing and shipping a few copies of the paperback, one to the Library of Canada, Legal Deposit, others to the authors.

www.ingramcontent.com/pod-product-compliance
Lightning Source LLC
Chambersburg PA
CBHW071601040426
42452CB00008B/1255